MENTAL
SYSTEMS
THEORY

4

JUAN MARTÍN FIGINI

MENTAL SYSTEMS THEORY

authorHOUSE®

AuthorHouse™
1663 Liberty Drive
Bloomington, IN 47403
www.authorhouse.com
Phone: 1-800-839-8640

Published by AuthorHouse   1/5/2012

ISBN: 978-1-4685-2432-1 (sc)
ISBN: 978-1-4685-2431-4 (hc)
ISBN: 978-1-4685-2430-7 (e)

Library of Congress Control Number: 2011962497

CONTENTS

Acknowledgements..ix

Preface...xi

Introduction...xiii

The Mental System..1

    Basic characteristics and interactions 1

    Laws of Interaction..10

Conclusion...71

Glossary 77

About The Author 85

ACKNOWLEDGEMENTS

To my wife and my family, for believing in me and for all their love.

To my friends, who express enormous affection for who I am and what I do.

To my patients, who fill me with gratification and joy in achieving their goals and their deepest desires.

To God for life, purpose, and his infinite love.

PREFACE

The Mental Systems Theory was created because I needed to understand myself in order to develop different solutions to several traumas I was suffering.

After years of research and reflection, I was able to finish this book, which is the first chapter of this philosophical theory about the mind.

I really enjoyed this process of creation and I love the idea that this work can help people to solve their mental and emotional problems.

This model can be applied in several fields and disciplines such as Business Administration, Psychology, Sociology, Education, Communication, Sports, Medicine, and more.

I believe that if we all achieve a better understanding of how our minds work we can find many solutions to a great number of problems in different areas of human manifestation.

Juan Martín Figini

Author

21/11/11

INTRODUCTION

The **Mental Systems Theory** was born with a clear purpose: to improve human beings' quality of life.

Towards this end, I spent years of research in the study of the human phenomenon, being able to find a fundamental premise: **both our emotional well-being and our whole reality are built around the thoughts we generate**. In turn, our thoughts are the emergent property of our belief system.

If this statement is true, is there a way to redefine our belief structure? If the answer is yes, what resources do we need to accomplish this task?

A resource that is a necessary condition for being able to define our particular way of being, is an understanding of how the mind works. And that is precisely what this book provides.

Both our emotional well-being and our whole reality are built around the thoughts we generate.

This work has been designed to offer the reader a model of the mind mechanism and its connections with the soul and the body.

To fulfill this purpose I have developed a set of concepts and laws which explain the mind phenomena.

I hope that the knowledge about mental systems offered by this book will be useful to understand the power we all have to design our lives.

THE MENTAL SYSTEM

Basic characteristics and interactions

A system is an entity whose existence and operations are justified as a whole through the interaction of its parts.[1] Following this definition, **the mental system** is an energy field of information whose existence and operations are justified as a whole through the interaction of the **mental sensory system** and the **belief system**.

All that is captured by the biological system of perception is then decoded by the brain in the form of electromagnetic waves. Those waves are then transmitted to the mental system.[2]

This input received by the mental system is captured by the mental sensory subsystem whose function is to transform the electromagnetic waves into sensory images, through the auditory, visual, tactile, olfactory, gustatory, and sensitive subsystems.[3]

---

1   Definition based on J. O'Connor and I. Mc Dermott, *Introduction to Systems Thinking*, Ediciones Urano, 1998, p. 27.

2   This premise can be inferred by the scientific discoveries of Gary Schwartz on the transmission and reception of electromagnetic waves through the human body. See L. Mc Taggart, *The intention experiment*, Editorial Sirio, 2007, p. 57-76.

3   The sensitive subsystem comprises all internal physical sensations. The sensory image, meanwhile, is a mental reproduction based on the senses of the biological system of perception.

The mental system is an energy field of information whose existence and operations are justified as a whole through the interaction of the **mental sensory system** and the **belief system.**

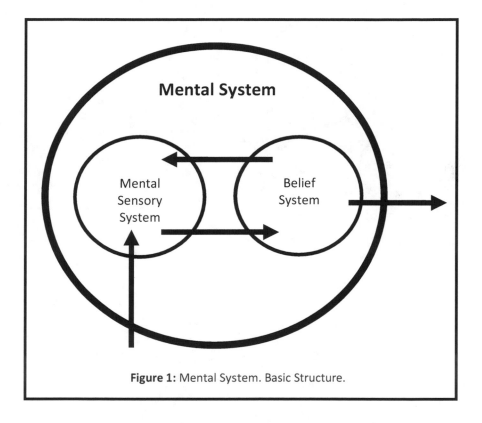

Figure 1: Mental System. Basic Structure.

The defining components of the mental sensory system are a reflection of the senses of the biological system of perception.

Biological perception is determined by the following senses: visual, auditory, tactile, gustatory, olfactory and sensitive.

The electromagnetic waves are captured by the mental sensory system, which transforms them into **sensory impressions**.

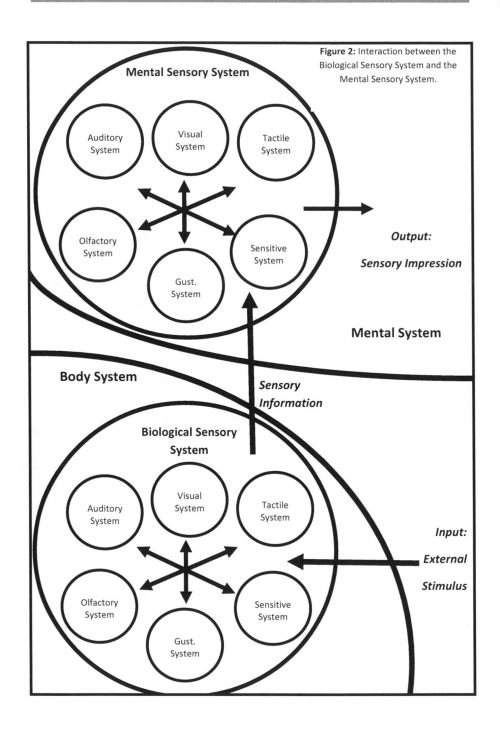

Figure 2: Interaction between the Biological Sensory System and the Mental Sensory System.

We shall illustrate these concepts with a simple **example**[4]:

If we are in a room, facing a blue wall, where we can hear a dog barking, it's hot and we smell food, all that sensory data that we have captured is happening in our mind.

How is this possible? Those external stimuli (light, sound, temperature and smell) have been received by our biological sensory system. Then, this information, has been processed by our brain, and transmitted in the form of electromagnetic waves into the mental sensory system. All the sensory images that we have mentioned (the blue wall, the heat, etc.) are the emerging data of this process.

In short, **all that we experience happens in our minds.**

Those **impressions**, which are the emerging property of the mental sensory system, are **sensory images with no linguistic meaning,** and they are later transmitted to the belief system.

The **belief system** is an entity whose existence and operations are justified as a whole through the interaction of beliefs.

When sensory impressions enter the belief system, a series of automatic connections between beliefs occurs, resulting in an emerging interpretation. It is worth noting that in this theory the concepts of interpretation and thought are use as synonymous.

---

4   For explanatory purposes, all the examples listed in this book constitute an oversimplification of the complexity of the mental phenomena, as the huge variety of variables make a full account of a case too difficult.

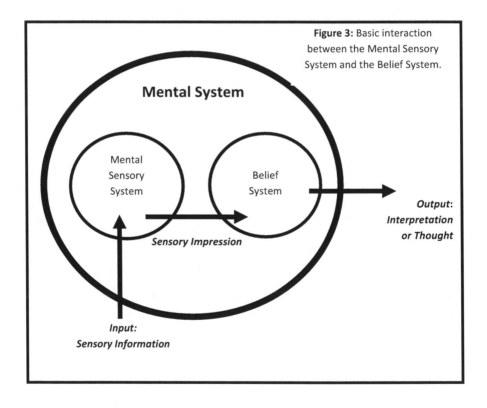

Figure 3: Basic interaction between the Mental Sensory System and the Belief System.

Mental System

Mental Sensory System

Belief System

Sensory Impression

Output: Interpretation or Thought

Input: Sensory Information

Beliefs are ideas that have a certain energetic charge and intensity and are firmly attached to the mind as truths.[5]

Ideas are sensory images with a certain linguistic meaning, composed of one or more words that assume a logical grammatical sense.

Returning to the example, if I am in the same room and I hear a dog barking, when this sensory impression enters the belief system it gets a linguistic meaning and the interpretation emerges: "A dog is barking".

Interpretations are ideas that have a certain energetic charge and intensity which generate an emotional effect on the body system.

Emotions are physical sensations produced by the energetic charge contained in the interpretation.

Beliefs are linked within the belief system through **the act of thinking**. Through the act of thinking, mental energy is directed towards a set of beliefs that form a network. Interpretations emerge from this association between beliefs.

---

5   The concept of belief applies to a gradual notion of truth, not an absolutist one. In this sense, we can understand the belief as an idea that has a certain degree of veracity.

Beliefs are ideas that have a specific energetic charge and intensity and have a certain degree of veracity.

Beliefs that are energetically **active** are those that can affect the thinking process and hence the resulting interpretations.

But there is also a huge set of **passive beliefs** which are in a potential state and therefore they do not affect the thinking process or its resulting interpretation.

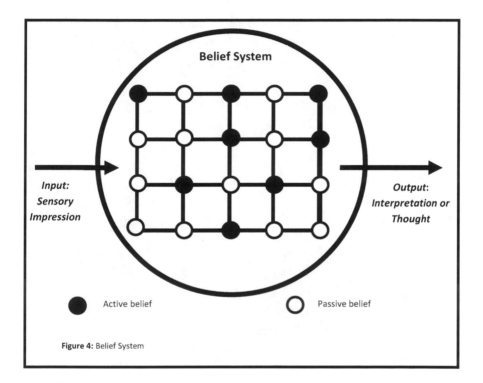

Figure 4: Belief System

Let's continue with the example:

If my belief system receives the sensory impression of the bark, and my related active beliefs at the moment are: "I need to study now to pass the test", "I need to concentrate", "if I fail my exam I will fall behind with my studies", "if I fall behind with my studies, my family will be mad at me" and so on, the resulting interpretation of my belief system at that moment, may be: "There is a dog barking. It is ruining my study time. This is harmful for me".

We can suppose that this thought has a negative energetic charge of a certain intensity level, and that it is transmitted in the form of electromagnetic waves into the body system, which processes it and generates a corresponding negative emotion.

LAWS OF INTERACTION

As has been mentioned before, the act of thinking involves addressing the mental energy to one or more beliefs. Active beliefs are those to which the dynamics of thinking has given a certain amount of mental energy that makes it possible for them to affect the resulting interpretation.

But this does not mean that those beliefs that are activated in the process of thinking are the only ones that exist.

All belief systems are complete. All possible beliefs exist and they are present in the mental space. We only need to address the mental energy to activate them and take them out of their passive state.

The premise that holds that belief systems have all conceivable beliefs at this level of evolution (whether they are active or not), is called the **law of completeness**.

Let us illustrate it with our example:

Just as my belief system has all those active beliefs mentioned before ("I need to study now for the test", "I need to concentrate", etc.), it also has other positive passive beliefs that can lead to a positive interpretation, such as: "I have all the knowledge, the available time and the ability to pass my exams", "any environment is favorable to my study process".

In turn, other passive negative beliefs also co-exist and they can generate an interpretation even more negative than the original one, such as: "I will never pass the test", "my family thinks I'm a failure".

LAW OF COMPLETENESS:

Each belief system has all active
and passive beliefs conceivable
at this level of evolution.

Although each belief system is complete, not all beliefs are affecting the thinking process. Those that are affecting it are considered active, and those that are not affecting it are considered passive.

The **thinking process** can be automatic or voluntary, generating a voluntary or an automatic interpretation, respectively, as an emergent property of the belief system.

An **automatic thought** is generated when an automatic link between beliefs occurs.

A **voluntary thought** is generated when a voluntary link between beliefs occurs.

The first type of thought is a reaction and the second type is a decided action guided by a purpose. The one who decides and guides the thinking process is our soul, what we are and will always be.

Continuing with our example:

If I let my automatic thinking process take place, the negative interpretation already mentioned will immediately emerge: "there is a dog barking, it is ruining my study time, this is harmful for me".

If, however, I voluntarily decide to intervene in the thinking process, I can activate any of the above mentioned positive passive beliefs, such as: "any environment is favorable to my study process", and thus I can voluntarily generate a positive thought: "even though the dog is barking, I can continue studying".

In this respect, the **soul** is a conscious energy that enjoys free will and operates on the mental system and on the body system.

It is the free will of the soul that makes it possible to choose which of the beliefs to activate in order to achieve the desired purpose.

This concept is key to understand how **human beings can voluntarily modify their personalities**, that is, their active belief systems.[6]

The soul is the one who can intervene in the thinking process to create a voluntary thought, and interrupt the chain of automatic thoughts.

In addition to free will, the soul has another faculty called **consciousness**, which consists of recognizing how the mental and the body system work.

---

6   To achieve this purpose the author of this book has developed Mental Systems Engineering, a discipline that applies the Mental Systems Theory principles and concepts, in order to align the human systems' belief structure with their desired state (in many cases that desired state is called health).

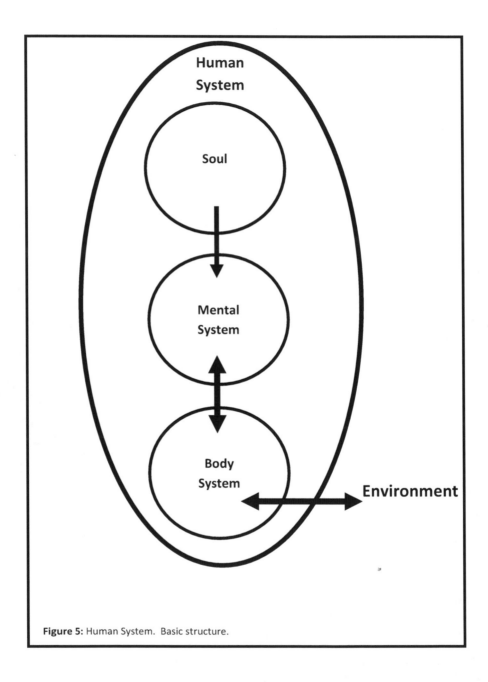

Figure 5: Human System. Basic structure.

The **soul** is a conscious energy that enjoys free will and operates on the mental system and on the body system.

As regards the mental system, there are **conscious and unconscious beliefs and thoughts**. The first ones are recognized by the soul and the second ones are not.

Moreover, there are conscious and unconscious emotions and behaviours.

All those beliefs and thoughts that are not recognized by the soul, constitute the **unconscious**.

Whether we are aware of our active beliefs or not, they are by definition susceptible of affecting the thinking process.

The belief system is always operating and automatically generating links, except when the soul deliberately intervenes in the dynamics of thinking.

It is worth noting that the process of automatic generation of thoughts occurs as long as the stimuli that feed it remain.

A **stimulus** is a sensory image of either internal or external origin.

In this sense, an **internal stimulus** is a sensory image that has been remembered or invented.

An **external stimulus** is a sensory image received from the environment.

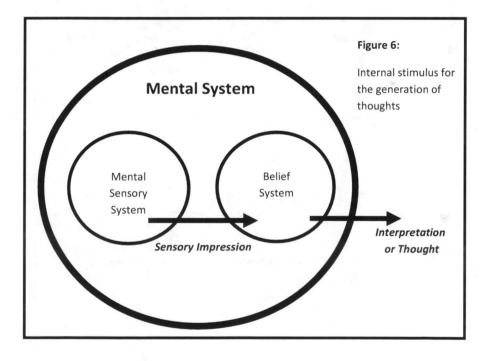

Figure 6:

Internal stimulus for the generation of thoughts

Mental System

Mental Sensory System

Belief System

Sensory Impression

Interpretation or Thought

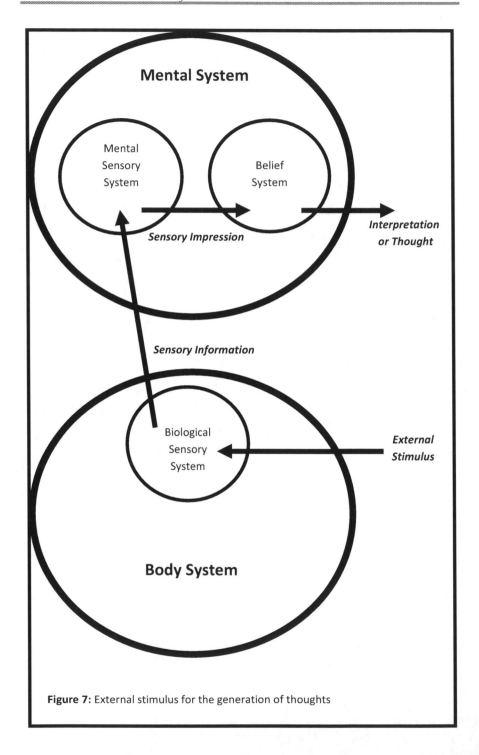

Figure 7: External stimulus for the generation of thoughts

External stimuli are captured by the biological system of perception and transformed into electromagnetic waves that eventually reach the mental system, where they are retransformed into sensory images.

It is worth pointing out that when we talk about a sensory image we are not only appealing to the visual sense, but also to the whole set of senses that constitute the sensory system and that are a reflection of the biological system of perception.

Internal stimuli are sensory images generated in the mental system. The thinking process is based on sensory images since all beliefs are formed by one or more sensory images endowed with linguistic meaning.

When we are thinking, we are activating and linking beliefs, and therefore, we are activating and associating a set of linguistic sensory images.

The thinking activity is a process undertaken jointly by the sensory system and the belief system. Mental energy takes the form of a sensory impression, which is then completed by the belief system with a linguistic meaning.

However, the belief system does not only operate when the person has incorporated language. From the moment the soul incarnates in the body system, a set of beliefs that constitute the **innate personality** is already active in the mental system.

That is why babies and children who have not yet learned any language can suffer disturbances in their emotional state as a result of their active innate beliefs. Children receive external stimuli, which are automatically decoded by the belief system, after they have assumed the character of a sensory impression.

The sensory impression receives a certain energetic charge and intensity from those innate beliefs; then, it is transformed into an interpretation and it is received by the body as a physical sensation. That physical sensation is the emotion, which can be either positive or negative, depending on whether the energetic charge of the interpretation is positive or negative, respectively.

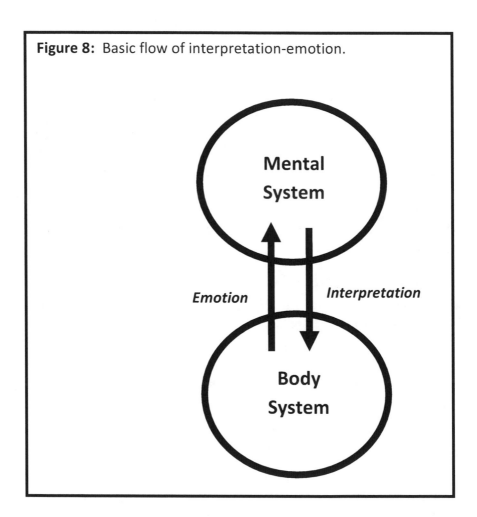

Figure 8: Basic flow of interpretation-emotion.

This is called the **law of correspondence**: every negative interpretation generates a negative emotion and every positive interpretation generates a positive emotion.

LAW OF CORRESPONDENCE:

Every negative interpretation
generates a negative emotion
and every positive interpretation
generates a positive emotion.

Continuing with our example:

When my body system receives the negative interpretation: "a dog is barking, it is ruining my study time, this is harmful for me", it consequently emits a negative emotion, such as "anger".

Similarly, if my body system receives the positive interpretation: "even though the dog is barking, I can continue studying", it emanates a positive emotion, such as "serenity".

The way in which the soul can become aware of what kind of energetic charge is prevailing in the thinking process is through emotion. Emotion is the indicator the soul has to understand whether positive or negative thoughts are taking place in the mental space. This recognition process is the outcome of the soul consciousness about the way the mental and the body system work. Being aware of what happens in our mental system is how we can voluntarily alter the course of thoughts in order to create a state of well-being or to break with the state of ill-being.

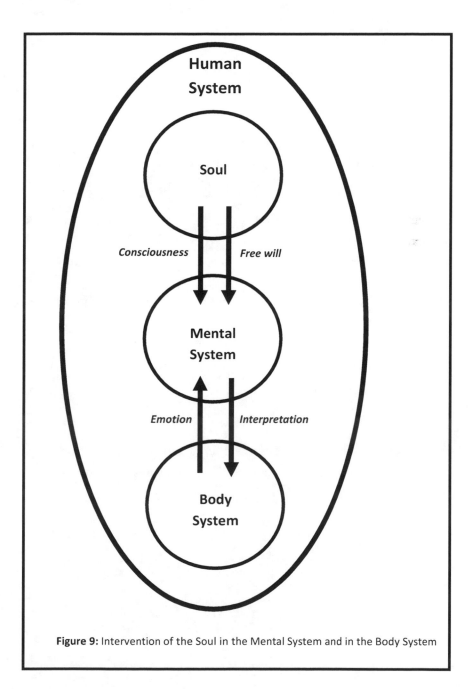

Figure 9: Intervention of the Soul in the Mental System and in the Body System

The degree of ill-being an individual suffers is equivalent to the intensity of the negative emotion manifested in the body.

Ill-being is the manifestation of any negative emotion, of any kind of intensity, such as: annoyance, hatred, anger, rage, anguish, sadness, depression, anxiety, fear, phobia, stress, etc.

Well-being is the manifestation of any positive emotion, of any kind of intensity, such as: relief, gladness, happiness, joy, excitement, peace, love, compassion, calmness, security, trust, etc.

In this regard, the intensity of an emotion is equivalent to the intensity of the interpretation that generates it.

This is precisely what the **law of proportional intensity** establishes: the energetic intensity of an emotion is equal to the energetic intensity of the interpretation that generates it.

Consequently, in our example we can deduce that the negative emotion "anger", of an energetic intensity grade four, is the effect of a negative interpretation: "this is harmful for me", of an energetic intensity grade four.

As a result of all laws mentioned above, it can be asserted that every emotion of a certain energetic charge and intensity has the same energetic charge and intensity of the interpretation that generates it.

LAW OF PROPORTIONAL INTENSITY:

The energetic intensity of an emotion is equal to the energetic intensity of the interpretation that generates it.

It is worth noting that the **energetic charge** is the energetic pole assumed by the interpretation as a result of the thinking process. The energetic charge can be either negative or positive, of varying degrees, ranging from absolute negativity to absolute positivity. When I speak of the degree of the positive or negative energy I am referring to the energetic intensity. **Energetic intensity** is the amount of mental energy that a belief, an interpretation or an emotion contains.

Let us suppose we have a scale of zero to ten in the negative pole, in which zero is no negativity and ten is absolute negativity. If we had a negative emotion "discomfort" of grade three, we would have a milder degree of suffering than in the case of a negative emotion "anger" of grade eight.

To suffer is to live a state of ill-being. In this sense, there are varying degrees of ill-being for the different intensities that negative emotions express in our bodies.

Everything I have described about negative emotions is the same for positive emotions. The greater the intensity of a positive emotion, the greater the level of well-being the person will experience.

Law of Intensity:

The higher the degree of frequency in
which a belief is recognized during
the thinking process, the higher its
energetic intensity; the lower the
degree of frequency in which a belief
is recognized during the thinking
process, the lower its energetic intensity.

The intensity of a negative emotion is equivalent to the intensity of the interpretation that generated it.

For example, if my positive interpretation is "yesterday I played football very well" of an intensity grade three, it will generate the positive emotion "gladness" of grade three.

Also, a positive interpretation "yesterday I played football wonderfully" of grade eight, will generate the positive emotion "happiness" of grade eight, which will cause a greater good than the first interpretation.

We know that interpretations are the result of an interaction between active beliefs. **The intensity and the charge of an interpretation are the result of the interaction between the intensities and charges of the different beliefs involved in the thinking process.**

The more frequently a belief participates in the thinking process, the higher its intensity level is.

This principle is called **law of intensity**: the higher the degree of frequency in which a belief is recognized during the thinking process, the higher its energetic intensity; the lower the degree of frequency in which a belief is recognized during the thinking process, the lower its energetic intensity.

LAW OF CERTAINTY:

The higher the intensity of a belief is, the higher the degree of certainty or veracity it expresses.

For example, if the belief "I am a productive person" activates twenty times during a day and the belief "I am a fun person" activates eight times during the same day, the first one will have a higher energetic intensity than the second one.

In the same way, if the belief "I cannot commit to anyone" activates thirty times in a week and the belief "nobody loves me" activates ten times in the same week, the first one will have a higher energetic intensity than the second one.

We know that beliefs are ideas that have a certain energetic charge and intensity and are firmly attached to the mind as truths. **The higher the intensity of a belief, the higher its level of veracity.**

This principle is called **law of certainty**: the higher the intensity of a belief, the higher the degree of certainty or veracity it expresses.

Following the example, due to its higher intensity, the belief "I am a productive person" has a higher veracity level than the belief "I am a fun person".

LAW OF INFLUENCE:

The higher the certainty level of a belief is, the greater its influence on the thinking process will be.

Beliefs are truths, and each one of them expresses a certain degree of veracity that is equivalent to its energetic intensity.

The higher the certainty level of a belief is, the greater its influence on the thinking process and thus on the resulting interpretation will be.

This is what the **law of influence** establishes: **the higher the certainty level of a belief is, the greater its influence on the thinking process will be.**

Therefore, according to our example, as the belief "I am a productive person" has a higher certainty level than the belief "I am a fun person", it will have a greater influence on the thinking process than the second one.

Let us suppose that we have to organize a party with our friends and there are different roles to fill. As my belief "I am a productive person" has more influence than the belief "I am a fun person", I will incline to choose operational tasks and not entertainment activities, based on the interpretation: "I am better at organizing than at entertaining".

All beliefs express a certain degree of veracity. Those beliefs that express more certainty will have the greatest influence on the resulting interpretation, and therefore, on our emotional state.

LAW OF INCONGRUITY:

When beliefs of opposite poles and different intensities interact with each other, they cause a decrease in the intensity of the belief which has a comparatively lower intensity and an increase in the one which has a comparatively higher intensity.

Interpretations are the result of an interaction between active beliefs. Some beliefs share the same energetic charge or pole, and others do not. When beliefs do not share the same pole, and have different intensities, the mental energy of the truth that has the relatively lower amount of energy decreases.

This is called the **law of incongruity**: when beliefs of opposite poles (incongruent) interact, they cause a decrease in the intensity of the truth that has a comparatively lower intensity.

This interaction also generates an increase in the intensity of the belief that has a comparatively higher intensity.

Let us suppose, for example, that we have a positive active belief "I am reliable" of an energetic intensity grade eight that interacts with a negative active belief "I get easily irritated", of an energetic intensity grade three. This interaction will cause an increase in the energy of the first belief, and a decrease in the second one.

On the contrary, if a negative active belief "I am an idiot" of an energetic intensity grade eight interacts with a positive active belief "I am brave" of an energetic intensity grade three, this would cause an increase in the amount of energy of the first belief and a decrease in the second one.

Law of Congruence:

When beliefs of identical poles interact with each other, they cause an increase in their respective intensities.

When beliefs of opposite poles but with equal intensities interact, they do not generate any decrease in their amounts of energy.

Then, for example, if the positive active belief "I am smart" of an energetic intensity grade seven interacts with the negative active belief "I am irresponsible" of an energetic intensity grade seven, this would not cause any alteration, because they have the same intensity.

When beliefs that have the same energetic charge interact with each other, their respective intensities increase.

This is precisely what the **law of congruence** states: when beliefs of identical poles (congruent) interact with each other, they cause an increase in their respective intensities.

Let us suppose that the positive active belief "all my children love me" of an energetic intensity grade four, interacts with the positive active belief "my husband loves me" of an energetic intensity grade seven, this will cause an increase in the amount of energy of both beliefs.

Similarly, if the negative active belief: "my neighborhood is unsafe" of an energetic intensity grade nine, interacts with the negative active belief "there are more and more diseases" of an energetic intensity grade five, this will generate an increase in the amount of energy of both beliefs.

It is worth mentioning that **when beliefs of identical poles and intensities interact with each other, their respective intensities also increase.**

We know then that beliefs interact with each other during the thinking process. This interaction generates increases and decreases in the intensity of one pole or the other.

The greater the frequency with which positive interpretations manifest, the more it means that positive beliefs are "winning the battle". This metaphor means that positive active truths have as a whole a strongest collective intensity than negative active truths.

The opposite can also happen. If negative interpretations and negative emotions manifested more often than the positive ones, the result would be a constant state of ill-being and suffering.

We know that beliefs are ideas that are firmly attached to the mind as truths. These truths can have either a positive or a negative charge of certain intensity. The energetic intensity of the belief is a result of its degree of participation in the thinking process. The more a belief is recognized, the more intense its charge will be.

We also know that the higher its intensity is, the higher its level of certainty will be; and that the higher its level of veracity is, the greater its influence on the act of thinking, and thus on interpretations will be.

When a positive interpretation emerges, we supposed that the charge and intensity of active positive beliefs have prevailed over the charge and intensity of negative active beliefs.

To illustrate with an example:

Let us suppose we had three active positive beliefs: "I am bold", "people love me", "I am good at my job", with a collective intensity of grade fourteen; and those beliefs interacted with three negative active beliefs: "I am afraid", "people do not understand me", "my job is too difficult for me", with a collective intensity of grade twelve. Since the intensity of positive beliefs would be higher than the intensity of negative beliefs, a positive interpretation would emerge: "since I am very appreciated and capable at work, I am thinking of asking for a promotion."

On the contrary, if those negative beliefs had a higher collective intensity than the positive ones, a negative interpretation would emerge, such as: "my job is too hard, I have to make a great effort for things to work out for me".

We know that an interpretation is a statement on the meaning of things. It is a set of sensory images with a certain linguistic meaning.

That linguistic meaning can, explicitly or implicitly, express either acceptance or rejection about the circumstances manifested in the sensory images.

If it expresses acceptance, the interpretation is positive. If it expresses rejection, the interpretation is negative.

Law of Acceptance and Rejection:

Every positive interpretation
corresponds with an idea of
acceptance about the circumstances
the interpretation refers to and every
negative interpretation corresponds
with an idea of rejection about
the circumstances mentioned
in the same interpretation.

What has been mentioned finds its place in the **law of acceptance and rejection**: every positive interpretation corresponds with an idea of acceptance about the circumstances the interpretation refers to and every negative interpretation corresponds with an idea of rejection about the circumstances mentioned in the same interpretation.

In that sense, **the whole emotional spectrum, from the negative pole to the positive pole, corresponds with a range of interpretation that goes from absolute rejection to complete acceptance, respectively.**

Let us suppose I had a positive interpretation "these holidays are great", which is supported by a set of sensory images, such as: "swimming in the sea on a hot day", "having dinner with my girlfriend in a luxury restaurant", "wake up in the morning in the hotel room with sunlight and the sound of the sea".

If the interpretation is positive, and we will discover it by the positive emotion it generates, we know by law that all these images that support the interpretation are accepted or approved.

The opposite would happen with a negative interpretation, such as: "these are the worst holidays of my life", supported by a set of sensory images: "when my car collided with a van and I hurt my chest and my neck", "staying at the hospital after the crash", "my wife saying that I'm a nuisance for the family". By law, all of these images are rejected or disapproved by me.

The whole emotional spectrum, from the negative pole to the positive pole, corresponds with a range of interpretation that goes from absolute rejection to complete acceptance, respectively.

Then, we understand that positive interpretations indicate acceptance of the circumstances they express and negative interpretations indicate rejection of the circumstances they express.

These circumstances are the sensory impressions that constitute the interpretation.

If the interpretation is negative it means the sensory impressions that entered the belief system favored the negative active beliefs over the positive active ones.

If the interpretation is positive it means the sensory impressions that entered the belief system favored the positive active beliefs over the negative active ones.

When a sensory impression favours a belief, it means that there is congruence between them. That congruence implies that the sensory impression is compatible with the sensory images that constitute the belief.

When a sensory impression does not favour a belief, it means that there is incongruity between them. That incongruity implies that the sensory impression is incompatible with the sensory images that constitute the belief.

Then, two things can happen: **sensory impressions can either validate or invalidate beliefs of positive or negative charge**. If positive beliefs are validated, the effect will be a positive interpretation, and therefore a positive emotion that indicates acceptance. If negative beliefs are validated, the effect will be a negative interpretation, and thus a negative emotion, indicative of rejection.

LAW OF RESONANCE AND DISSONANCE:

Sensory impressions that validate a belief - and therefore are resonant with it- generate an increase in its amount of energy. On the contrary, sensory impressions that invalidate a belief - and therefore are dissonant with it- generate a decrease in its amount of energy.

This concept of validation or invalidation finds its expression through the **law of resonance and dissonance:** those sensory impressions that are recognized by a belief can have two types of effects, resonance or dissonance. The first one implies that the belief finds a sensory validation that causes an increase in its amount of energy. The second one implies that the belief finds a sensory invalidation that causes a decrease in its amount of energy.

Let us suppose we have a positive active belief "all parents are loving", which consists of the sensory image of "a father hugging his son". If the sensory image of "a father beating his son" entered, that belief would lose energy, since the new sensory image would invalidate it and would generate a dissonance with the image that constitutes the belief.

On the other hand, if another sensory image of "a father hugging his son" entered, it would cause a validation of the positive belief: "all parents are loving", since it would be compatible with the image that constitutes it.

Following the example, let us suppose we also have an active negative belief that says "all parents do harm", which consists of the sensory image of "a father hitting his son".

If we saw a recent situation in which a father were beating his son, the negative belief would be validated by that new sensory impression.

On the contrary, if we received a sensory image in which a father were hugging his son, this would invalidate the negative belief "all parents do harm", since it would be incompatible with the sensory image that constitutes it.

LAW OF SENSORY DISTORTION:

Active beliefs may unconsciously influence sensory impressions by removing and/or adding sensory data.

Necessarily, when a belief increases its amount of energy, there is another one or other ones that decrease theirs. **Since belief systems are complete, when a sensory impression validates a set of beliefs, it also invalidates those beliefs that are inconsistent with the first set.**

The belief system is constantly receiving internal and external stimuli, and the amounts of energy are constantly being redistributed between beliefs.

However, the relationship between the sensory system and the belief system is bidirectional. This means that **sensory impressions affect beliefs and also beliefs affect sensory impressions.**

How beliefs affect sensory impressions can be explained by the **law of sensory distortion.**

Active beliefs may unconsciously distort sensory impressions in three possible ways:

1. When one or more sensory data -that did not exist- are added to the original sensory impression.

2. When some sensory data are removed from the original sensory impression.

3. When some sensory data are erased from the original sensory impression, and some others are added to it.

In order to get a better understanding of these filters, let us see the following examples:

In the first case, let us suppose a woman has the belief: "everyone wants to abuse me". During a meeting, this lady turns and slaps the man that was sitting behind her, saying: "don't touch me". The innocent man replies: "I didn't touch you and honestly, I do not want to have a relationship with a crazy woman".

The origin of this situation is that the lady has added a sensory piece of information (tactile) that did not exist in the original sensory impression.

In the second case, a mother has the belief: "my son is very correct". One day this "correct son" hits the teacher in the stomach in front of his mother. The teacher approaches the woman and asks her: "aren't you going to do anything about it?" and the lady replies, "why?" The teacher says in anger: "Your son beat me in front of you". The mother of this "sweet child" answers: "I will not let you blame my son for your personal problems, he is an exemplary and well-educated person, and he would be incapable to do such thing, I will report you to the principal".

Notably, this lady was influenced by her belief in such way that she lost contact with the original (visual) sensory information.

Regarding the third filter, let us take for example the case of a young man who has the belief: "no one appreciates me". While he is walking through a campus corridor, one teacher says to the other "he's five foot tall". But the student hears: "he's a fool boy".

In this case, what happened was that his negative belief "no one appreciates me" altered the original (auditory) sensory impression by removing and adding sensory data that did not correspond with what actually occurred.

It is worth noting that the original sensory impression is the one that proceeds without distortion from the mental sensory system to the belief system.

Then, sensory impressions can be altered within the belief system.

Knowing this, it makes sense to claim that **our sensory reality is strongly conditioned by our active belief system**.

It may happen that we perceived what beliefs approve and could not perceive what beliefs disapprove. That is why sometimes it is so important to verify our memories with another person who has experienced the same event. The disgrace would be that both of us shared the same sensory distortion.

We know then that active beliefs can be validated or invalidated by the sensory impressions received by the system. Also, active beliefs of a higher intensity can alter the flow of sensory information. Original sensory images can suffer this alteration by the addition and/or removal of data.

The emergent property of this process of mutual influence between the mental sensory system and the belief system is the interpretation.

We have seen that an interpretation emotionally affects the body system. **The emotion on the body system takes place in the vital energy system.**[7]

The vital energy system receives this energetic charge of the interpretation, causing a physical sensation that is equivalent to the pole of the interpretation.

The positive pole favours the free movement of energy. The negative pole interrupts the movement of energy.[8]

If these blockages in the energy system are not solved in time, they can produce negative changes in the other subsystems that constitute the body and cause, in the worst case scenario, serious physical diseases.

Negative emotions are not only capable of generating major disruptions in the body system but also affect a person's behaviour.

All negative emotions generate behavioural dispositions that tend to harm the person who suffers them and his or her environment.

7   The concept of "vital energy system" comes from Chinese Traditional Medicine. It is defined as a set of circuits or meridians through which the energy that feeds the body organs flows. This knowledge provides the basis for acupuncture and other related techniques.
8   Gary Craig, author of the Emotional Freedom Techniques argues that "every negative emotion is caused by a blockage in the human body's energy system." Reference: www.emofree.com

On the contrary, all positive emotions generate behavioural dispositions that tend to favour that person's well-being and his or her environment.

We define **behaviour** as a physical and/or linguistic action that affects reality.

Positive behaviour is a physical and/or linguistic positive action that affects reality. It is sustained by a positive emotion, and therefore, it is guided by a positive interpretation.

Negative behaviour is a physical and/or linguistic negative action that affects reality. It is sustained by a negative emotion, and therefore, it is guided by a negative interpretation.

Positive behaviours are the ones that tend to increase the well-being of the person who adopts them and of his or her environment.

Negative behaviours are the ones that tend to increase the ill-being of the person who adopts them and of his or her environment.

For example, if someone at work generates the negative thought: "my boss does not appreciate me", which causes him a negative emotion of "anguish", is very likely that he spends his working day mistreating his colleagues and customers. Thus, he will harm himself, his colleagues and the company.

On the contrary, if that person generates at work the positive thought: "I love my job", and therefore the positive emotion of "happiness", he will tend to have a good relationship with his co-workers and will become more efficient and effective at his tasks, favouring the labour environment and company's performance.

In summary, positive interpretations cause positive emotions, which consequently tend to generate positive behaviours.

Negative interpretations cause negative emotions, which tend to generate negative behaviours.

Behaviour, by definition, creates new realities. Any alteration of reality generated by behaviour is defined as a **result**.

A result can be negative or positive depending on how it is interpreted.

For example, I can interpret that paying my taxes results in a waste of my money. That thought produces a negative emotion in me, and therefore we can see that it is a negative interpretation. This result, evaluated from this interpretation, will then seem negative.

Instead, if I interpret that the result of paying my taxes is an act of social and moral commitment to the country, I might generate a positive emotion, and therefore the interpretation would be positive. This result, evaluated from this interpretation, will then seem positive.

Results often operate as sensory stimuli of validation for the beliefs that originated them.

In that case, **a circuit of validation is formed, that starts with beliefs and it is reinforced by the results generated by those same beliefs**.

Let us suppose that a set of positive beliefs express a positive interpretation, which consequently causes a positive emotional state.

This sequence generates positive behaviour and hence a result that validates those positive beliefs that originated this chain of cause and effect. The result itself is neither positive nor negative, but it turns out to be positive because it reinforces the positive pole of thinking.

This new stimulus reinforces the circle of belief-outcome until the soul voluntarily breaks it or new sensory data enter and interrupt the energetic pole of the circle.

What I have stated finds its expression in the **law of open virtuous**

circles: an open virtuous circle occurs when positive active beliefs are able to surpass negative active beliefs in intensity, generating a sequence of positive interpretations, emotions, behavior and results that present a sensory validation to the same positive beliefs that generated the results; and thus an open virtuous circle between positive beliefs and positive results is established.

This law can be illustrated by the following example: a person has a positive active belief that says "all the people who know me, love me", therefore in his circle of friends he emits the following thought: "my friends love me", which generates the positive emotion of "affection". Consequently, he greets everyone with a hug; generating in his friends a big hug in return. This result constitutes for that person a validation of the original belief, and restarts then the virtuous circle.

Law of Open Virtuous Circles:

Positive active beliefs that surpass negative active beliefs in intensity, generate a sequence of positive interpretations-emotions-behaviour, that causes a positive result that presents a sensory validation to the positive beliefs that originated this circuit.

Figure 10:
Open virtuous circle.

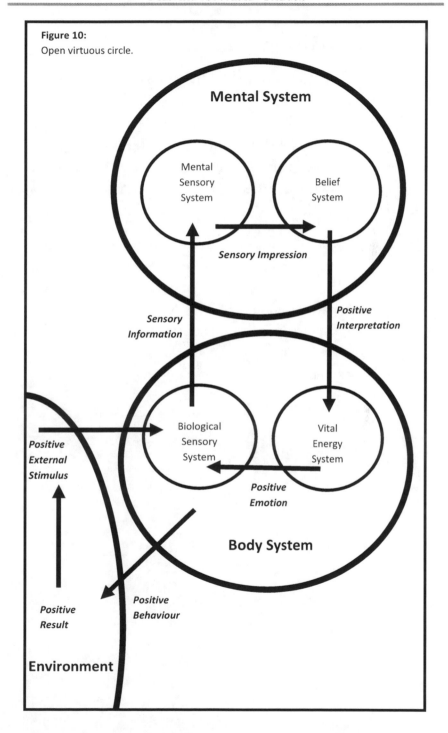

Exactly the opposite happens when an open vicious circle is built between negative beliefs and negative results.

This phenomenon is explained by the **law of open vicious circles**: an open vicious circle occurs when negative active beliefs are able to surpass positive active beliefs in intensity, generating a sequence of negative interpretations, emotions, behaviour and results that present a sensory validation to the same negative beliefs that generated the results; and thus an open vicious circle between negative beliefs and negative results is established.

An example of an open vicious circle is that of a person with the negative active belief: "everyone wants to attack me", therefore in his circle of friends he emits the following thought: "my friends mock me", which causes him the negative emotion of "rage". Subsequently, he decides to bother them with aggressive jokes, generating an equivalent response from them. This result constitutes for that person a validation of the original belief, and restarts then the vicious circle.

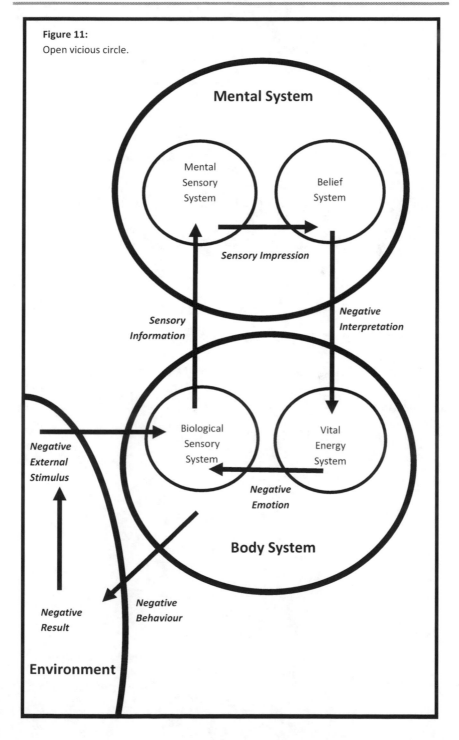

Figure 11:
Open vicious circle.

Law of Open Vicious Circles:

Negative active beliefs that surpass positive active beliefs in intensity, generate a sequence of negative interpretations-emotions-behaviour, that causes a negative result that presents a sensory validation to the negative beliefs that originated this circuit.

The laws of open virtuous and vicious circles, try to give an explanation for the two possible types of open feedback.

An **open feedback** occurs when the active beliefs that originate the cycle are repeatedly reinforced by the results they generate.

A **closed feedback**, on the other hand, takes place when active beliefs are reinforced repeatedly by the interpretations they generate.

According to these concepts, I will state the **law of closed virtuous circles**: a closed virtuous circle occurs when positive active beliefs are able to surpass negative active beliefs in intensity, generating positive interpretations, which will validate the same positive beliefs that originated them.

Thus, a closed virtuous circle is built between positive beliefs and positive interpretations.

It is worth noting that the closed virtuous circle tends to increase the energetic intensity of positive beliefs and positive interpretations.

For example, a person who goes running every day has the active positive belief: "I'm constantly improving myself", so he emits the positive thought: "every time I go running, I gain more endurance", which generates the emotion of: "satisfaction". In this way, he validates the original positive belief and begins a new closed virtuous circle.

LAW OF CLOSED VIRTUOUS CIRCLES:

Positive active beliefs that surpass negative active beliefs in intensity, generate a sequence of positive interpretation-emotion, that validates the original positive beliefs.

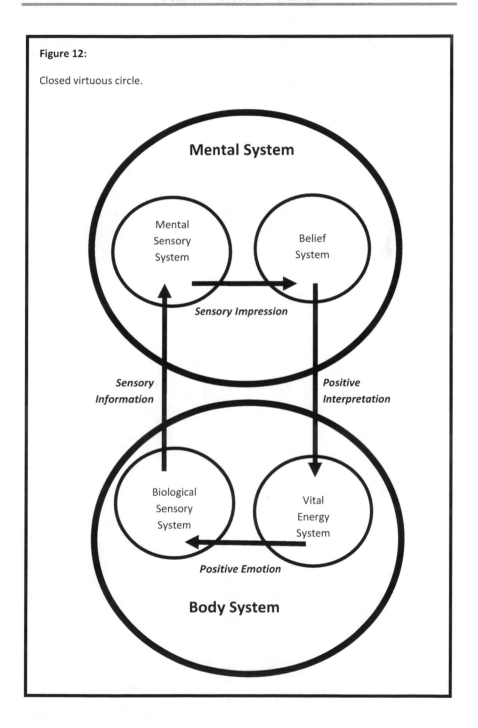

Figure 12:

Closed virtuous circle.

Exactly the opposite happens when a closed feedback takes place between negative beliefs and negative interpretations.

This phenomenon is explained by the **law of closed vicious circles**: a closed vicious circle occurs when negative active beliefs are able to surpass positive active beliefs in intensity, generating negative interpretations, which will validate the same negative beliefs that originated them. Thus, a closed vicious circle is built between negative beliefs and negative interpretations.

It is worth pointing out that the closed vicious circle tends to increase the energetic intensity of negative beliefs and negative interpretations.

We can see here the example of someone who does not engage in any physical activity and has the negative active belief: "I'm bad at sports", so he emits the negative thought: "it doesn't make sense to exercise". This creates the negative emotion of "annoyance", which validates the original negative belief, restarting the closed vicious circle.

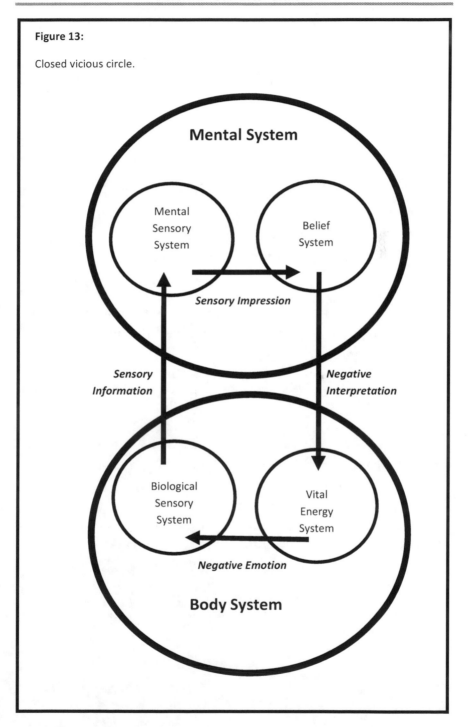

Figure 13:

Closed vicious circle.

Then, from these assumptions we know that beliefs can be validated and reinforced by open and closed feedback.

When it comes to an open circle, beliefs are validated and reinforced by results.

When it comes to a closed circle, beliefs are validated and reinforced by interpretations and emotions.

As regards behaviour, it produces new realities for human beings. These new realities constitute new learning opportunities. Learning is the result of associating a sensory impression to a linguistic meaning. We could say that learning consists of providing language to the perceived reality.

What has been mentioned finds its expression in the **law of linguistic meaning**: all sensory impressions are provided with linguistic meaning by the act of thinking.

The soul may or may not be aware of the meaning that is given to the sensory image.

In short, beliefs provide meaning to all the events in our lives. Let us remember that all sensory impressions enter the general belief system, and at that moment a series of connections between beliefs occurs, creating a type of thought that brings meaning to what is happening.

The meaning that is provided has a linguistic nature.

Law of Linguistic Meaning:

All sensory impressions are
provided with linguistic meaning
by the act of thinking.

Language, as any other piece of information, already exists in the general belief system of any human system. According to the law of completeness that was stated at the beginning of this book, all conceivable beliefs in this life are already present in the general belief system. All we need is to remember in order to activate those beliefs that were in a passive state, or to remember in order to recognize those beliefs that are in an active state.

The new sensory impressions with a given linguistic meaning are the ones I define as **experiences**. These, in turn, constitute the source of information that keeps a record of what we perceive in our lives, that is our **memory**.

It is worth noting that **all beliefs are different pieces of information**. In this sense, all the information on the past, the present and the future is expressed through beliefs.

There are beliefs about the past, the present and the future. For example: "I played football last week", is a belief about the past. "I play football" is a belief about the present. "I will play football next Saturday" is a belief about the future.

When we want to remember an experience, what we do is to automatically invoke those beliefs that constitute that experience.

Experiences are images from the past that sustain positive and negative beliefs.

It may happen that the images of the past that feed negative beliefs are traumatic.

The images of these beliefs possess such a high negative intensity that they are constantly affecting the thinking process.

According to the law of influence, those negative beliefs with a high level of intensity, that is a high level of veracity, strongly condition the act of thinking.

Thus, the emerging thoughts of the mental system are negative, and they possess a high energetic intensity. The way of noticing a **trauma** is to pay attention to the images about the past that sustain the emerging negative interpretation.

Of course, the way of becoming aware of the negative state of thought is through the negative emotion that is expressed in the body.

In general, trauma is expressed through vicious circles. Negative beliefs achieve a certain level of intensity that allows interpretations or results to be traumatic.

In this regard, it is necessary to neutralize the vicious circle and to release the energetic intensity of those negative beliefs that constitute the trauma.

Sometimes experiences help to activate beliefs that were in a passive state, other times they intensify some beliefs that were already activated.

Our different experiences affect our active belief structure and thus our personality can be modified over time.

We are born with a certain personality, but it changes along with the different experiences we go through.

There are human systems whose personalities are functional to achieve their desired state, and that enable them to live in a healthy condition.

But there are also human systems whose personalities are dysfunctional to achieve their desired state, and that lead them to a state of ill-being.

Therefore, it is very important to know how to identify negative beliefs and how to identify and strengthen the positive functional beliefs that can generate the personality the human system needs to achieve its desired goals.

In general, these desires are expressed by the soul, but the personality does not allow them to be realized.

Just in case I will define the human system, so there is no confusion. A **human system** is an entity whose existence and operations are justified as a whole through the interaction of the soul, the mental system and the body system.

There are two types of human systems: **individual and collective**.

The first ones are human beings. The second ones are communities.

Communities are groups of individuals who share a collective personality and pursue certain ends. These ends may or may not be aligned with the collective desire of the souls that constitute the community.

The challenge is to understand which active belief system defines the personality of the community that is being analyzed.

The **human system** is an entity whose existence and operations are justified as a whole through the interaction of the soul, the mental system and the body system.

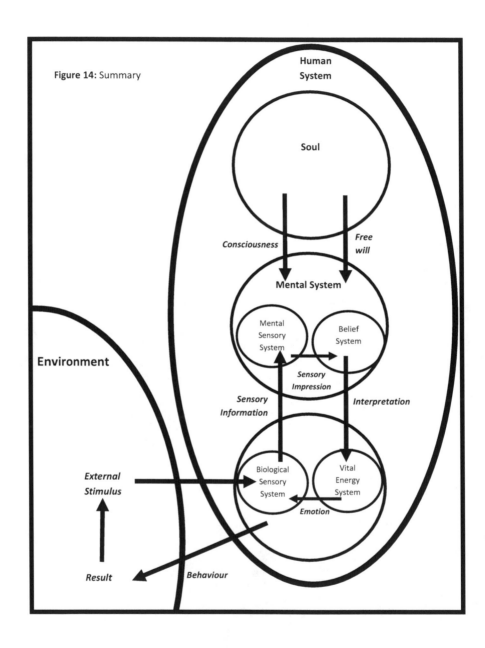

Figure 14: Summary

There are different types of communities of different sizes and different personalities.

When I speak of communities I refer to sports teams, companies, universities, non-governmental organizations or nations, among others.

In all these cases **Mental Systems Engineering**˙ is the discipline that enables us to make a diagnosis of the active belief system and to operate on it to produce the changes in the personality that the human system needs.

Before the end of this book I would like to clarify an idea that I have implicitly expressed at the beginning. **The mind is not the brain**. They are two different phenomena. They are linked but they are not identical.[9]

The mind is an energy field of information that receives electromagnetic waves emitted by the brain.

And in turn the mind emits thoughts which are electromagnetic waves that affect the vital energy system causing all kind of feelings or emotions.

In fact, we could suppose that there is a parallelism between the neural networks formed in the brain and the belief networks constituted in the mind.

Many unanswered questions remain; a lot of work is to be done.

This book is the first stage of study on mental systems. The ramifications of this essay on other research areas will be developed later.

---

9   See E. Laszlo, *The Creative Cosmos*. Editorial Kairós, 1997, p. 148.

CONCLUSION

Here ends the first stage of study on mental systems. Through this work I have devoted myself to the analysis of the mind mechanism and its connections to the soul and the body.

In addition, I have developed a set of concepts and laws that clearly explain the mental phenomena.

If we manage to understand these laws in depth, we will be able to voluntarily create the appropriate pattern of thought that help us fulfil our purposes.

Besides the theory, we need a method that allows us to apply its principles. In order to do so, I have created **Mental Systems Engineering**, a discipline that aims to understand and to operate on the mental system, in order to align the human system's belief structure with its desired state.

This can be accomplished as long as the soul is able to express itself through the personality.

We know that personality is the active belief system. There are some beliefs that predominate over others. They prevail because they possess a comparatively higher energetic intensity.

Mental Systems Engineering is a discipline that aims to understand and to operate on the mental system, in order to align the human system's belief structure with its desired state.

If those beliefs are negative, it is most likely that the human system suffers from a negative emotional state that makes it unable to live its desired situation. But if it could voluntarily alter the course of the thinking process and thus begin to give more intensity to the positive beliefs over the negative ones, it could generate a state of well-being, favourable to achieve a desired result.

Every human system, either an individual or a community, has a personality. If that personality enables the soul to express its purpose, then the human system will be able to conquer its possibility of realization.

In times like this, when mankind is moving towards a paradigm shift, it is appropriate to provide cognitive tools that help us walk the path of evolution in the best possible way.

Let us be then the voluntary expression of the best beliefs that exist in our mental system.

Let us be the voluntary expression
of the best beliefs that exist
in our mental system.

GLOSSARY

Ability: Behavioural disposition that allows the person to achieve a goal.

Active beliefs: A set of beliefs which affect the thinking process, and therefore, the resulting interpretations.

Automatic behaviour: Behaviour produced by an automatic thought.

Automatic thought: The emerging property of the automatic link between beliefs.

Behaviour: A physical and/or linguistic action that affects reality.

Belief: An idea that has a certain energetic charge and intensity and possesses a certain amount of veracity.

Belief system: An entity whose existence and operations are justified as a whole through the interaction of beliefs.

Biological sensory system: An entity whose existence and operations are justified as a whole through the interaction of the biological auditory, visual, tactile, olfactory, gustatory, and sensitive systems. A set of biological senses that capture the stimuli coming from the environment.

Closed feedback: A dynamic that takes place when certain active beliefs are repeatedly reinforced by the interpretations they generate.

Community: A collective human system. A group of individuals who share a collective personality and pursue certain ends. These ends may or may not be aligned with the collective desire of the souls that constitute the community.

Conscious active beliefs: All the active beliefs that are recognized by the soul.

Conscious emotions: All the emotions that are recognized by the soul.

Consciousness: An ability of the soul, which consists of recognizing how the mental system and the body system work.

Emotion: A physical sensation produced by the energetic charge contained in the interpretation.

Energetic charge: The energetic pole assumed by the belief, the interpretation and the emotion.

Energetic intensity: The amount of mental energy that a belief, an interpretation or an emotion contains.

Experience: One or more sensory images received from the environment with a given linguistic meaning.

External stimulus: A sensory image received from the environment.

Feedback: A dynamic that occurs when a cause generates an effect, which in turn reinforces the cause that originated it.

Free will: The ability of the soul to choose between different ways of expression.

Human system: An entity whose existence and operations are justified as a whole through the interaction of the soul, the mental system and the body system.

Idea: One or more sensory images with a certain linguistic meaning composed of one or more words that assume a logical grammatical sense.

Ill-being: The manifestation of any negative emotion, of any kind of intensity.

Internal stimulus: A sensory image that has been remembered or invented.

Interpretation: An idea that has a certain energetic charge and intensity which generates an emotional effect on the body system. It's the emergent property of the belief system and the mental system.

Learning: The act and result of associating a sensory impression with a linguistic meaning. The act and result of recognizing active beliefs and of activating and recognizing passive beliefs.

Memory: A source of information that keeps a record of what we perceive in our lives.

Mental sensory system: A subsystem that belongs to the mental system. An entity whose existence and operations are justified as a whole through the interaction of the auditory, visual, tactile, olfactory, gustatory, and sensitive systems. It is the entity in charge of capturing the sensory biological information and transforming it into sensory images.

Mental system: An entity whose existence and operations are justified as a whole through the interaction of the mental sensory system and the belief system.

Negative behaviour: A physical and/or linguistic negative action that affects reality.

Negative belief: An idea that has a negative energetic charge of certain intensity and possesses a certain amount of veracity.

Negative emotion: A negative physical sensation produced by the negative energetic charge contained in the interpretation.

Negative energetic charge: The negative energetic pole assumed by the belief, the interpretation and the emotion.

Negative interpretation: An idea that has a negative energetic charge of certain intensity which generates a negative emotional effect on the body system.

Open feedback: A dynamic that occurs when certain active beliefs are repeatedly reinforced by the results they generate.

Passive beliefs: A set of beliefs which are in a potential state and therefore they do not affect the thinking process or its resulting interpretation.

Personality: An active belief system.

Positive behaviour: A physical and/or linguistic positive action that affects reality.

Positive belief: An idea that has a positive energetic charge of certain intensity and possesses a certain amount of veracity.

Positive emotion: A positive physical sensation produced by the positive energetic charge contained in the interpretation.

Positive energetic charge: The positive energetic pole assumed by the belief, the interpretation and the emotion.

Positive interpretation: An idea that has a positive energetic charge of certain intensity which generates a positive emotional effect on the body system.

Result: Any alteration of reality generated by behaviour.

Sensory image / Sensory impression: Mental sensory reproduction based on the senses of the biological system of perception that has no linguistic meaning.

Soul: Conscious energy that enjoys free will and operates on the mental system and on the body system.

Stimulus: A sensory image of either internal or external origin.

Suffering: Ill-being.

System: An entity whose existence and operations are justified as a whole through the interaction of its parts.

Think: To direct mental energy towards one or more beliefs. The act of associating beliefs.

Thought: Interpretation.

Trauma: A set of images about the past that sustain one or more negative beliefs, which frequently affect the thinking process and turn out to be the basis of the sensory impressions that feed an emerging negative interpretation.

Unconscious: A set of beliefs and thoughts that are not recognize by the soul.

Unconscious active beliefs: All the active beliefs that are not recognized by the soul.

Unconscious behaviour: A behaviour that is not recognized by the soul.

Unconscious emotions: All the emotions that are not recognized by the soul.

Unconscious thought: A thought that is not recognized by the soul.

Vital energy system: An entity whose existence and operations are justified as a whole through the interaction of the vital energy circuits of the body system.

Voluntary behaviour: Behaviour produced by a voluntary thought.

Voluntary thought: The emerging property of the voluntary link between beliefs.

Well-being: The manifestation of any positive emotion, of any kind of intensity.

Index of Figures

Figure 1: Mental System. Basic Structure 3

Figure 2: Interaction between the Biological Sensory System
and the Mental Sensory System 4

Figure 3: Basic interaction between the Mental Sensory System and the Belief System 6

Figure 4: Belief System 9

Figure 5: Human System. Basic Structure 14

Figure 6: Internal stimulus for the generation of thoughts 17

Figure 7: External stimulus for the generation of thoughts..............19

Figure 8: Basic flow of interpretation-emotion 20

Figure 9: Intervention of the Soul in the Mental System and
in the Body System 23

Figure 10: Open virtuous circle 53

Figure 11: Open vicious circle 55

Figure 12: Closed virtuous circle.........................59

Figure 13: Closed vicious circle.........................61

Figure 14: Summary 68

ABOUT THE AUTHOR

Juan Martín Figini is the creator of the **Mental Systems Theory**˙ and the **Mental Systems Engineering**˙. His career has been focused on the understanding and development of human beings in society.

As the **Director** of **IBG Human Development**˙, he has designed and applied several training programmes based on Mental Systems Engineering, such as "Conscious Leadership", "Mental Training for Athletes", "Vocational Development", "Personal Evolution" and "Mental Training for Managers and Executives", among others.

He worked as a **Consultant** for **Manchester Business School**, The University of Manchester, UK.

He was the Executive Director of "Young Leadership and Country Vision", a cultural and social project which was part of an international social movement launched by Imagine Chicago. Following this initiative he organized and directed, among others, a free seminar for more than 120 young people, that offered one of the best programmes in the world on leadership development: Self Managing Leadership. This program was created by Brian Bacon and it is offered by the Oxford Leadership Academy.

He has a **Degree in Political Science** from **Saint Andrew's University** (Argentina). His degree thesis, titled: *Alienation in Rousseau: Social*

Criticism and Pedagogical Project, received from the academic jury of Saint Andrew's University the maximum score of ten points. He also studied the **International Relations Degree** in that university.

He was granted a complete scholarship by the **Weatherhead School of Business**, Case Western Reserve University, USA, for the Post-graduate Degree: Appreciative Inquiry Certificate in Positive Business and Society Change.

He has a Post-graduate Degree in Models and Tools of Ontological Coaching from the University of Buenos Aires (Argentina), and a Post-graduate Degree in Techniques and Dynamics of Coaching Intervention from the University of Buenos Aires (Argentina). He holds a Master's Degree in Neuro-Linguistic Programming, from the Southern Institute of NLP, The Society of NLP, International NLP, (USA). He received the International Certificate in Coaching from the International Coaching Community (ICC). He was certified in the Fundamental Course and the Advance Level of the Emotional Freedom Techniques (EFT), from the EFT Certificate of Completion Program (USA).

He also studied the courses: "Phenomenology of intersubjectivity and its importance for the understanding of mental illness", Faculty of Philosophy, Catholic University (Argentina); "I, subject and identity; the birth of these concepts in the modern ages (XVII and XVIII centuries)", Faculty of Philosophy, Catholic University (Argentina); "The way of being of the human subject in the philosophy of Kant and Hegel", Faculty of Philosophy, Catholic University (Argentina).

For more information:

www.imaginebeinggreater.com

4